TWO, FOUR, SIX, EIGHT

FAT-QUARTER QUILTS YOU'LL APPRECIATE

COMPILED BY *Lissa Alexander*

Martingale
Create with Confidence

Moda All-Stars
Two, Four, Six, Eight: Fat-Quarter Quilts You'll Appreciate
© 2020 by Martingale®

Martingale®
19021 120th Ave. NE, Ste. 102
Bothell, WA 98011-9511 USA
ShopMartingale.com

Printed in China
25 24 23 22 21 20   8 7 6 5 4 3 2 1

Library of Congress Cataloging-in-Publication Data is available upon request.

ISBN: 978-1-68356-055-5

MISSION STATEMENT

We empower makers who use fabric and yarn to make life more enjoyable.

CREDITS

**PUBLISHER AND
CHIEF VISIONARY OFFICER**
Jennifer Erbe Keltner

CONTENT DIRECTOR
Karen Costello Soltys

DESIGN MANAGER
Adrienne Smitke

MANAGING EDITOR
Tina Cook

PRODUCTION MANAGER
Regina Girard

**ACQUISITIONS AND
DEVELOPMENT EDITOR**
Laurie Baker

**COVER AND
BOOK DESIGNER**
Kathy Kotomaimoce

TECHNICAL EDITOR
Carolyn Beam

PHOTOGRAPHERS
Adam Albright
Brent Kane

COPY EDITOR
Melissa Bryan

ILLUSTRATOR
Sandy Loi

SPECIAL THANKS
*Photography for this book was taken at
the homes of Jodi Allen in Woodinville, Washington,
Libby Warnken in Ankeny, Iowa, and at Lori Clark's
The Farmhouse Cottage in Snohomish, Washington.*

Contents

Introduction

Give a shout, give a cheer, for fat quarters, bring 'em here!

It's true. Just when you thought your fabric stash was big enough, you found yourself picking up a few more fat quarters (FQs) of fabric you couldn't live without. These 18" x 21" pieces of fabric call out from quilt-shop shelves: *Pick me! Take me home! You don't have one like this. Ooh, these four look great together. What could you make with them?*

Yep, we've all been there. But sometimes you need just the right pattern to put those FQs to work once they've been "on the bench" in your stash for a while. *Two, Four, Six, Eight: Fat-Quarter Quilts You'll Appreciate* to the rescue! Inside you'll find a dozen new patterns you can use to turn those FQs into something even more fabulous. Whether you have 2 FQs or 32 FQs, there's a pattern here from a Moda All-Star designer that will be a game changer for you.

We think these dozen designers are at the top of their class. Have fun "studying" their personal fun facts to learn a bit more about them. And while you're at it, see which team we've assigned them to captain. It's all in good fun, which we know you'll have as you dive into your stash of FQs (seriously though, if you need to go out and find all-new FQs, who's stopping you? Not us!)

And in keeping with our motto of doing good with the Moda All-Star series of books, royalties for this book will be donated to Special Olympics (SpecialOlympics.org), an international organization that changes lives by promoting understanding, acceptance, and inclusion between people with and without intellectual disabilities. Through sports, Special Olympics athletes are seeing themselves for their abilities, not disabilities. That's something we can all cheer for!

~ Lissa Alexander

First Down

VANESSA GOERTZEN

FAT QUARTERS

FINISHED QUILT
68½" × 68½"

FINISHED BLOCK
14" × 14"

Get in the game with eight of your favorite fat quarters and a background, combining them to make an easy-to-piece throw that's perfect for wrapping up in. Whether you see a tree farm of tall pine trees growing this way and that or arrows pointing toward a first down, the stands are sure to be filled with admirers of your clever patchwork. Score!

MATERIALS

Yardage is based on 42"-wide fabric. Fat quarters measure 18" × 21".

8 assorted fat quarters (Vanessa used 2 red prints, 2 black prints, 2 aqua prints, 1 green print, and 1 white with red stripe) for blocks
3¾ yards of white print for blocks and border
⅝ yard of green print for trees
⅝ yard of red with white stripe for binding
4⅝ yards of fabric for backing
77" × 77" piece of batting

CUTTING

All measurements include ¼" seam allowances.

From *each* of the fat quarters, cut:
2 rectangles, 2½" × 14½" (16 total)
2 rectangles, 2½" × 12½" (16 total)
2 rectangles, 2½" × 10½" (16 total)
2 rectangles, 2½" × 8½" (16 total)

From the white print, cut:
26 strips, 2½" × 42"; crosscut into:
  ☻ 16 rectangles, 2½" × 12½"
  ☻ 16 rectangles, 2½" × 10½"
  ☻ 32 rectangles, 2½" × 8½"
  ☻ 128 squares, 2½" × 2½"
8 strips, 6½" × 42"

From the green print for trees, cut:
8 strips, 2½" × 42"; crosscut into 64 rectangles, 2½" × 4½"

From the red with white stripe for binding, cut:
8 strips, 2½" × 42"

MAKING THE BLOCKS

Press the seam allowances as indicated by the arrows.

1 Draw a diagonal line on the wrong side of the white squares. Layer a marked square on one end of a green 2½" × 4½" rectangle, right sides together. Sew on the drawn line. Trim ¼" beyond the

Designed and pieced by *Vanessa Goertzen*; quilted by *Marion Bott*

line and press the corner open. Repeat with another marked square on the opposite end to make a flying-geese unit that measures 2½" × 4½", including seam allowances. Make 64 units.

Make 64 units,
2½" × 4½".

2 To make one block, gather the following pieces:
- ✪ 4 flying-geese units
- ✪ 2 white 2½" × 8½" rectangles
- ✪ 1 white 2½" × 10½" rectangle
- ✪ 1 white 2½" × 12½" rectangle
- ✪ matching print 2½" × 8½" and 2½" × 10½" rectangles
- ✪ matching print 2½" × 12½" and 2½" × 14½" rectangles

3 Sew the four flying-geese units together to make a unit that measures 4½" × 8½", including seam allowances. Make 16 units.

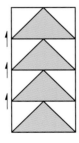

Make 16 units,
4½" × 8½".

4 Sew white 2½" × 8½" rectangles to both long sides of a unit from step 3 to make a unit that measures 8½" square, including seam allowances. Make 16 units.

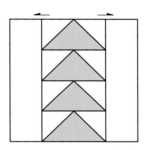

Make 16 units,
8½" × 8½".

5 Sew a print 2½" × 8½" rectangle to the left edge of a unit from step 4, and then sew a matching 2½" × 10½" rectangle to the top. This unit should measure 10½" square, including seam allowances. Make 16 units.

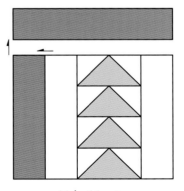

Make 16 units,
10½" × 10½".

Hey hey, ho ho, this tree farm quilt is on the grow! What a great crop of trees **Vanessa Goertzen** cultivated from her stash of FQs. She's planted all sorts of fun quilting ideas in our heads. We're naming Vanessa captain of the Sowing Squad (punny, right?)!

If I'm perusing fat quarters in a quilt shop, I'm likely to purchase a dozen. Even if I don't have a specific plan for them, I want to make sure I have a good mix for any future project.

If my high school had been made up entirely of quilters, they'd have voted me most likely to finish my homework early!

When I have scraps left over from fat quarters, I use them in a quilt backing or give them away.

If quilting were a team sport, I'd be captain of the Quilting Speed Demons Club.

When it's game time in my sewing room and I have to get serious about quilting, my go-to snacks are Storck Riesen candies or Red Vines.

In high school, the activities I was most involved with were tennis, track, and a cappella choir.

Two, four, six, eight, who do you appreciate when it comes time to make a quilt? My mom! She lives a block away and is always happy to help with the kids when deadlines loom.

Fat quarters score a perfect 10 because they can be adapted to almost any quilt pattern— a perfect substitute for yardage!

Name two, four, six, or yes, even eight things you couldn't live without in your quilting studio: A design wall, a comfy chair, true-crime podcasts, and treats.

  LellaBoutique.blogspot.com

6 Sew a white 2½" × 10½" rectangle to the left edge of a unit from step 5, and then sew a white 2½" × 12½" rectangle to the top. The unit should measure 12½" square, including seam allowances. Make 16 units.

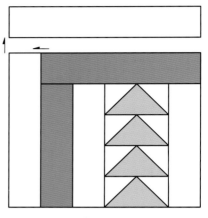

Make 16 units,
12½" × 12½".

7 Sew a print 2½" × 12½" rectangle to the left edge of a unit from step 6, and then sew a matching 2½" × 14½" rectangle to the top to make a block that measures 14½" square, including seam allowances. Repeat to make a total of 16 blocks.

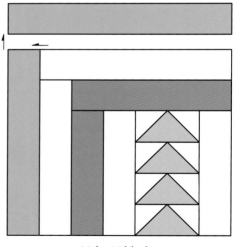

Make 16 blocks,
14½" × 14½".

ASSEMBLING THE QUILT TOP

1 Referring to the quilt assembly diagram on page 11, arrange the blocks in four rows of four blocks each, rotating the blocks as shown. Sew the blocks into rows; join the rows. The quilt top should measure 56½" square, including seam allowances.

Quilt assembly

2 Sew the white 6½"-wide strips together end to end. Cut two strips, 56½" long, and sew them to opposite sides of the quilt top. Press seam allowances toward the border. Cut two strips, 68½" long, and sew them to the top and bottom of the quilt. Press seam allowances toward the border. The quilt top should measure 68½" square.

FINISHING THE QUILT

For more details on any of the finishing steps, go to ShopMartingale.com/HowtoQuilt to download free illustrated information.

1 Layer the quilt top, batting, and backing; baste the layers together.

2 Quilt by hand or machine. The quilt shown is machine quilted with an allover framed flower design.

3 Trim the excess batting and backing. Use the red 2½"-wide strips to make double-fold binding, and then attach the binding to the quilt.

Sew, Team, Sew!

ME AND MY SISTER DESIGNS

FAT QUARTERS

FINISHED CADDY
9½" × 17"

Designed by *Me and My Sister Designs*;
pieced and quilted by *Mary Jacobson*

You'll be cheering when you no longer have to search to find your scissors, seam ripper, or rotary cutter! This cute-as-can-be sewing caddy takes just two fat quarters and a small amount of sewing time, and voilà! You have a mat to soften the vibration of your sewing machine **and** *corral the tools you need to keep at hand. Useful and pretty—what could be better!*

MATERIALS

Fat quarters measure 18" × 21".

1 fat quarter of pink floral for front and back
1 fat quarter of pink check for pocket and binding
10" × 17½" piece of batting
Temporary fabric adhesive spray (optional)

CUTTING

All measurements include ¼" seam allowances.

From the pink floral, cut:
2 rectangles, 10" × 17½"

From the pink check, cut:
1 square, 10" × 10"
4 strips, 2" × 21"

MAKING THE SEWING CADDY

Press the seam allowances as indicated by the arrows. For more details on basting, quilting, binding, or other techniques, go to ShopMartingale.com/HowtoQuilt to download free illustrated information.

1 Layer a pink floral rectangle, right side *down*, the batting, and then the second pink floral rectangle, right side *up*. Baste the layers using temporary fabric adhesive or the method of your choice. Quilt by hand or machine. The sewing caddy shown was machine quilted with diagonal lines to form a diamond pattern. Trim to 9½" × 17".

2 Fold the pink check square in half, wrong sides together, to make the pocket. Center the pocket on one end of the quilted rectangle, aligning the bottom raw edges. The pocket will extend ¼" beyond the quilted rectangle on both sides. To secure the pocket, stitch three lines from the pocket fold to the raw edges: one line through the center and then ¼" from the center on both sides, backstitching at each end.

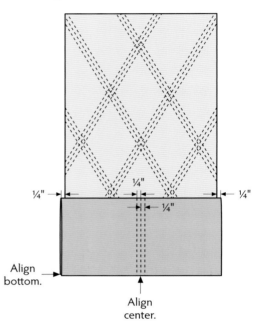

3 Align the ends of the pocket with each side of the quilted rectangle and pin in place. Create a tuck halfway between one side and the center by pinching the extra pocket fabric together along the

raw edges. Repeat to make a second tuck on the other side of the center. Pin the tucks in place and then baste ⅛" from all raw edges.

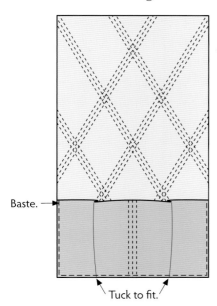

Baste.

Tuck to fit.

FINISHING THE CADDY

Use the pink check 2"-wide strips to make double-fold binding, and then attach the binding to the caddy. Place your sewing machine on the quilted end and let the pocket end hang in front of your sewing table. Use the pockets to keep your most frequently used sewing tools close at hand.

Game On!

SHERRI McCONNELL

FINISHED TABLE RUNNER
19½" × 58½"

FINISHED BLOCK
12" × 12"

You've gotta love a quilt that can do double duty. So if it's game night at your place more often than not, consider using the quilt as a mini wall hanging instead of as a table runner. Either way, it's so fun to make, you may want to add additional hearts—one for every member of your family. It's sure to be a favorite.

MATERIALS

Yardage is based on 42"-wide fabric. Fat quarters measure 18" × 21".

3 fat quarters: 1 *each* of medium blue, red, and navy prints, for blocks
1 fat quarter of white print for sashing and inner border
⅝ yard of white solid for block backgrounds
⅜ yard of navy floral for outer border
⅜ yard of medium blue print for binding
1¾ yards of fabric for backing
24" × 63" piece of batting

CUTTING

All measurements include ¼" seam allowances.

From the medium blue print, cut:
8 squares, 4" × 4"

From the red print, cut:
8 strips, 2" × 21"

From the navy print, cut:
8 rectangles, 3½" × 6½"

From the white print, cut:
6 strips, 1½" × 21"
5 rectangles, 1½" × 12½"

From the white solid, cut:
1 strip, 4" × 42"; crosscut into 8 squares, 4" × 4"
1 strip, 3½" × 42"; crosscut into 8 squares, 3½" × 3½"
4 strips, 2" × 42"; crosscut into 8 strips, 2" × 21"
1 strip, 1½" × 42"; crosscut into 16 squares, 1½" × 1½"

From the navy floral, cut:
4 strips, 3" × 42"

From the medium blue print for binding, cut:
5 strips, 2¼" × 42"

Designed by *Sherri McConnell;* quilted by *Marion Bott*

MAKING THE BLOCKS

Press the seam allowances as indicated by the arrows.

1 Draw a diagonal line on the wrong side of the white solid 4" squares. Layer a marked square on a medium blue 4" square, right sides together. Sew ¼" on each side of the marked line. Cut on the drawn line to make two half-square-triangle units for block corners. Trim each unit to 3½" square, including seam allowances. Repeat to make 16 corner units.

Make 16 units.

2 Sew red print and white solid 2"-wide strips together in pairs to make eight strip sets, 3½" × 21". Crosscut a total of 16 segments, 3½" wide, and 32 segments, 2" wide.

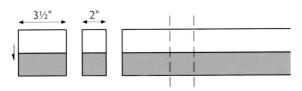

Make 8 strip sets, 3½" × 21".
Cut 16 segments, 3½" × 3½", and 32 segments, 2" × 3½".

3 Sew 2" segments to opposite sides of a 3½" segment, reversing the color placement, to make a side unit that measures 3½" × 6½", including seam allowances. Make 16 side units.

 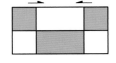

Make 16 units,
3½" × 6½".

4 Draw a diagonal line on the wrong side of the white solid 3½" squares. Layer a marked square on one end of a navy print 3½" × 6½" rectangle, right sides together. Sew on the drawn line. Trim the seam allowances to ¼" and press the corner open. Repeat to make four units and four reversed units that measure 3½" × 6½", including seam allowances.

Make 4 of each unit,
3½" × 6½".

5 Draw a diagonal line on the wrong side of the white solid 1½" squares. Layer a marked square on the upper-left corner of a unit from step 4, right sides together. Sew on the drawn line. Trim the seam allowances to ¼" and press the corner open. Repeat on the upper-right corner to make a heart unit. Repeat to make four units and four reversed units that measure 3½" × 6½", including seam allowances.

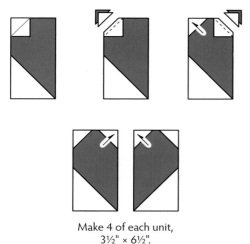

Make 4 of each unit,
3½" × 6½".

6 Join the units from step 5 to make a heart unit that measures 6½" square, including seam allowances. Make four.

Make 4 units,
6½" × 6½".

7 Arrange four corner units, four side units, and one heart unit into three rows. Sew the units into rows; join the rows to make a block that measures 12½" square, including seam allowances. Make four blocks.

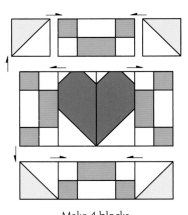

Make 4 blocks,
12½" × 12½".

ASSEMBLING THE TABLE RUNNER

1 Sew the blocks and white print 1½" × 12½" sashing strips together in alternating positions. The table-runner center should measure 12½" × 53½", including seam allowances.

2 Sew the white print 1½"-wide strips together end to end. Cut into two strips, 53½" long. Sew these to the long edges of the table runner. The table runner should measure 14½" × 53½", including seam allowances.

3 Sew three navy floral 3"-wide strips together end to end. From this strip, cut two strips, 58½" long. Cut the remaining navy strip into two pieces, 3" × 14½". Sew these shorter strips to the ends of the table runner. Sew the 58½"-long strips to the long edges of the table runner. The table runner should measure 19½" × 58½".

FINISHING THE TABLE RUNNER

For more details on any of the finishing steps, go to ShopMartingale.com/HowtoQuilt to download free illustrated information.

1 Layer the runner top, batting, and backing; baste the layers together.

2 Quilt by hand or machine. The table runner shown is machine quilted with an allover curlicue design.

3 Trim the excess batting and backing. Use the medium blue 2¼"-wide strips to make double-fold binding, and then attach the binding to the table runner.

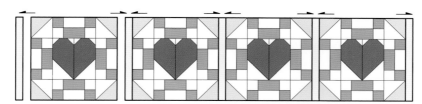

Table-runner assembly

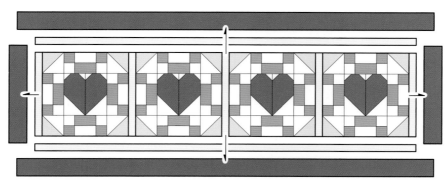

Adding borders

Golden Rule

LISA BONGEAN

08 FAT QUARTERS

FINISHED QUILT
40½" × 40½"

Here's the ticket to happiness—be kind. It might be a short take on the full Golden Rule, but it's advice we can't be too often reminded of. A little flannel patchwork, a bit of appliqué, all accented by a hint of stitchery . . . remember to say "thank you" when you're raking in the compliments!

MATERIALS

Yardage is based on 42"-wide fabric. Fat quarters measure 18"×21".

1¾ yards of cream print flannel for center block, outer border, and binding

½ yard of dark gray print flannel (A) for strips and inner border

7 fat quarters of assorted print flannels for strips and appliqué: 3 medium gray (A–C), 3 dark gray (B–D), and 1 cream plaid

1 fat quarter of dark gray hand-dyed felted wool for vines and stems

2¾ yards of fabric for backing

44" × 44" piece of batting

1⅔ yards of 12"-wide paper-backed fusible web

Pearl cotton, size 5, in ecru, light gray, dark gray, and variegated black

Fabric pencil or water-soluble marker

Light box (optional)

CUTTING

All measurements include ¼" seam allowances.

From the cream print, cut:

1 strip, 21" × 42"; crosscut into 1 square, 21" × 21"

4 strips, 5" × 42"; crosscut into:
- ✿ 2 strips, 5" × 40½"
- ✿ 2 strips, 5" × 31½"

5 strips, 2½" × 42"

From dark gray A, cut:

8 strips, 1¾" × 42"; crosscut into:
- ✿ 2 strips, 1¾" × 31½"
- ✿ 2 strips, 1¾" × 29"
- ✿ 2 strips, 1¾" × 22½"
- ✿ 2 strips, 1¾" × 20½"

From medium gray A, cut:

4 strips, 1¾" × 19½"

From dark gray B, cut:

4 strips, 1¾" × 17½"

From the cream plaid, cut:

4 strips, 1¾" × 15½"

Continued on page 24

Continued from page 23

From dark gray C, cut:
4 strips, 1¾" × 13½"

From medium gray B, cut:
4 strips, 1¾" × 11½"

From dark gray D, cut:
4 strips, 1¾" × 9½"

From medium gray C, cut:
4 strips, 2½" × 6½"

MAKING THE CENTER BLOCK

For more information on appliqué and embroidery techniques, go to ShopMartingale.com/HowtoQuilt.

1 Make a full-size copy of the center-block appliqué and embroidery placement diagram, located on page 31, by copying the diagram four times and taping the sections together. Fold the cream print 21" square in half both vertically and horizontally, and lightly crease the folds. Use a light box or window to mark the position of the vines, leaves, and flowers. Trace *Be Kind* in the center. Using the patterns on page 30, prepare the leaves, flowers, and buds for fusible appliqué. Following the manufacturer's instructions, iron fusible web to the wrong side of the dark gray wool. Cut 12 strips, ³⁄₁₆" × 20", for the vines and 14 strips, ⅛" × 20", for the stems.

2 Use black pearl cotton and a stem stitch to fill in the letters. Use a Colonial knot to dot the letter *i* in *Kind*.

3 Referring to the photo on page 25 and the appliqué and embroidery placement diagram, position and fuse the prepared shapes. Arrange and fuse the vines and stems first, cutting to length as needed. Use matching pearl cotton and a blanket

stitch to appliqué the flowers, leaves, and buds, and use a cross-stitch for the vines. Add Colonial knots in black pearl cotton for the berries.

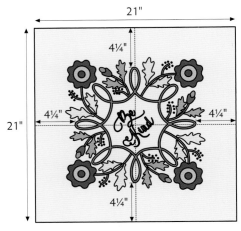

Appliqué and embroidery placement

4 Trim the completed center block to 20½" square, including seam allowances.

ASSEMBLING THE QUILT CENTER

Press the seam allowances as indicated by the arrows.

1 Fold the dark gray A 1¾" × 22½" and 1¾" × 20½" strips in half lengthwise and gently crease the folds. Sew the 20½"-long strips to opposite sides of the quilt center. Center the 22½"-long strips and sew them to the remaining two sides.

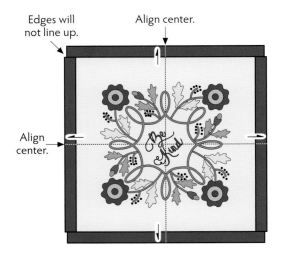

Edges will not line up.
Align center.
Align center.

Designed by *Lisa Bongean*

Big G, little o: Go! Go! **Lisa Bongean** is speedy, precise, and practicing what she preaches. She's the powerhouse behind Primitive Gatherings. With a good reminder to us all to be kind, we're naming Lisa captain of the Congeniality Club!

If I'm perusing fat quarters in a quilt shop, I'm likely to purchase every one that I like!

In high school, I was voted most likely to become a workaholic.

When I have scraps left over from fat quarters, I save them for another quilt.

If quilting were a team sport, I'd be captain of the Half-Square-Triangle Squad.

When it's game time in my sewing room and I have to get serious about quilting, my go-to snack is Dove dark chocolate.

In high school, the activities I was most involved with were volleyball and softball.

Now that I'm out of high school, the club I WISH quilters had today is the Teeny-Tiny Pieces Club.

Two, four, six, eight, who do you appreciate when it comes time to make a quilt? I L-O-V-E my machine quilters!

Fat quarters score a perfect 10 because there is usually fabric left over that can be used in another quilt.

Name two, four, six, or yes, even eight things you couldn't live without in your quilting studio: Netflix or audiobooks, Beam n Read personal light, Juki sewing machine, Olfa 60 mm rotary cutter, Aurifil thread for machine stitching, Valdani thread for hand stitching, Martelli tweezers, and Dovo scissors.

 LisaBongean.com

2 Fold the 1¾"-wide strips of medium gray A and B, dark gray B through D, cream plaid, and 2½"-wide strips of medium gray C in half lengthwise and gently crease the folds. Matching the center creases, sew two medium gray A strips to opposite sides of the quilt center, and then sew two medium gray A strips to the remaining two sides. Continue in this manner to add strips in the following order: dark gray B, cream plaid, dark gray C, medium gray B, dark gray D, and medium gray C. Trim the quilt center to 29" square, including seam allowances.

Align centers.

Trim to 29" × 29".

ADDING THE BORDERS

1 Sew the dark gray A 1¾" × 29" strips to opposite sides of the quilt center. Sew the dark gray A 1¾" × 31½" strips to the top and bottom. The quilt top should measure 31½" square, including seam allowances.

2 Sew the cream print 5" × 31½" strips to opposite sides of the quilt top. Sew the cream print 5" × 40½" strips to the top and bottom. The quilt top should measure 40½" square.

3 Using the patterns on page 29, trace the numbers for the year onto the bottom border, centering the numbers. Numbers 0–9 are included so you can customize your own year. Use black pearl cotton and a stem stitch to fill in the numbers.

Quilt assembly

4 Referring to the photo and the appliqué placement diagram, position and fuse the remaining prepared shapes to the cream outer border. Arrange and fuse the vines and stems first, cutting to length as needed. Use matching pearl cotton and a blanket stitch to appliqué the flowers, leaves, and buds, and use a cross-stitch for the vines and stems. Add Colonial knots in black pearl cotton for the berries.

FINISHING THE QUILT

For more details on any of the finishing steps, go to ShopMartingale.com/HowtoQuilt to download free illustrated information.

1 Layer the quilt top, batting, and backing; baste the layers together.

2 Quilt by hand or machine. The quilt shown is machine quilted with a pebble stitch and swirls in the center block and outer border. Two straight lines are quilted in each of the patchwork strips.

3 Trim the excess batting and backing. Use the cream 2½"-wide strips to make double-fold binding, and then attach the binding to the quilt.

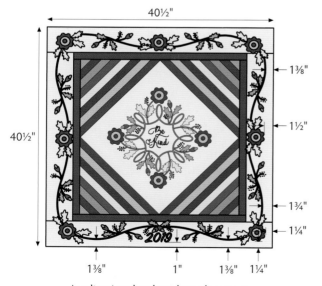

Appliqué and embroidery placement

Stem stitch outline, and fill with stem stitch.

Embroidery pattern

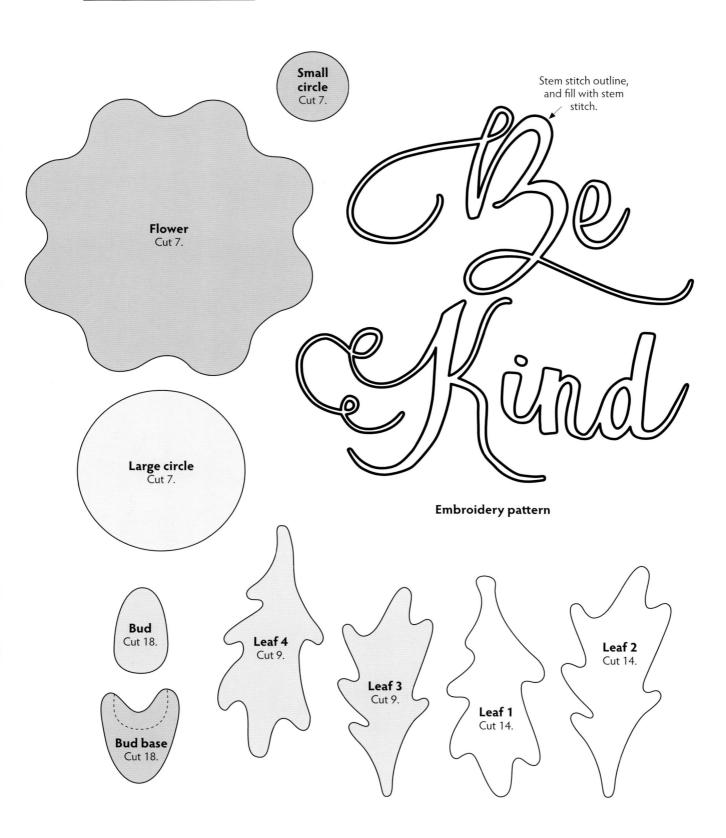

Appliqué patterns do not include seam allowances and are reversed for fusible appliqué.

Small circle Cut 7.

Flower Cut 7.

Stem stitch outline, and fill with stem stitch.

Large circle Cut 7.

Embroidery pattern

Bud Cut 18.

Leaf 4 Cut 9.

Leaf 3 Cut 9.

Leaf 1 Cut 14.

Leaf 2 Cut 14.

Bud base Cut 18.

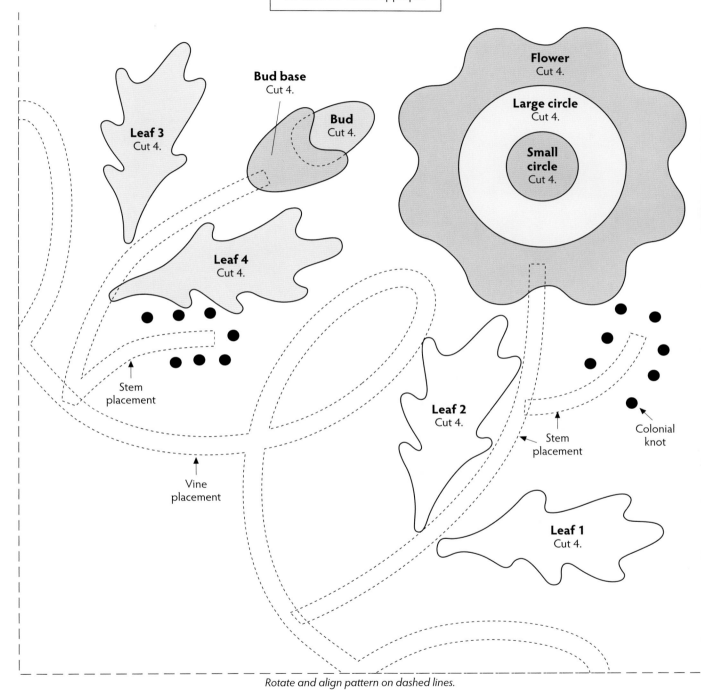

Appliqué patterns do not include seam allowances and are reversed for fusible appliqué.

Flower Cut 4.

Large circle Cut 4.

Small circle Cut 4.

Bud base Cut 4.

Bud Cut 4.

Leaf 3 Cut 4.

Leaf 4 Cut 4.

Stem placement

Vine placement

Leaf 2 Cut 4.

Leaf 1 Cut 4.

Stem placement

Colonial knot

Rotate and align pattern on dashed lines.

Center-block appliqué patterns and embroidery placement

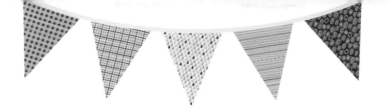

Rookie Vibe

SANDY GERVAIS

FAT QUARTERS

FINISHED QUILT
42½" × 51½"

The vote is in for Rookie of the Year and we're all atwitter. This project is perfect for the little one in your life (and for a beginning quiltmaker ready to show off her newly discovered hobby). The quilt will look equally charming displayed on a wall, draped over a crib rail, or snuggled under by a tiny tot.

MATERIALS

Yardage is based on 42"-wide fabric. Fat quarters measure 18" × 21".

6 fat quarters of assorted blue and green prints
   (A–F) for houses, bird appliqués, and border
1⅝ yards of white tone on tone for background
½ yard of blue-and-green plaid for bias binding
2⅞ yards of fabric for backing
49" × 58" piece of batting
1 button, ¼" diameter, for bird's eye (optional)
Template plastic *OR* EZ Quilting Tri-Recs rulers
Supplies for appliqué method of your choice

CUTTING

All measurements include ¼" seam allowances.
Use the patterns on page 39 to make plastic templates for the pennant triangle and half triangle. Or, you may use the Tri-Recs rulers to cut these shapes.

From print A, cut:
1 rectangle, 8½" × 11½" (house 1)
1 rectangle, 3½" × 6½" (roof 4)
1 pennant triangle

From print B, cut:
1 rectangle, 6½" × 14½" (house 2)
1 rectangle, 4" × 7½" (roof 6)
1 pennant triangle

From print C, cut:
1 rectangle, 7½" × 10½" (house 3)
1 rectangle, 4½" × 8½" (roof 5)
1 pennant triangle

From print D, cut:
1 rectangle, 6½" × 18½" (house 4)
1 rectangle, 4½" × 8½" (roof 1)
1 pennant triangle

From print E, cut:
1 rectangle, 8½" × 13½" (house 5)
1 rectangle, 4" × 7½" (roof 3)
1 pennant triangle

From print F, cut:
1 rectangle, 7½" × 9½" (house 6)
1 rectangle, 3½" × 6½" (roof 2)
2 pennant triangles

Continued on page 34

Continued from page 33

From the white tone on tone, cut:
2 strips, 21½" × 42"; crosscut 1 strip into:
- ✿ 1 rectangle, 21½" × 24½"
- ✿ 1 rectangle, 7½" × 9"
- ✿ 1 rectangle, 7½" × 8"
- ✿ 1 rectangle, 6½" × 8½"
- ✿ 1 rectangle, 4½" × 8½"
- ✿ 1 rectangle, 4½" × 6½"

Crosscut the second strip into:
- ✿ 1 rectangle, 21½" × 24½"
- ✿ 3 strips, 6½" × 17"; cut into 6 triangles, 1 half triangle, and 1 half triangle reversed

1 strip, 4½" × 42"; crosscut into:
- 4 squares, 4½" × 4½"
- 4 squares, 4" × 4"

1 strip, 3½" × 42"; crosscut into 4 squares, 3½" × 3½"

From the blue-and-green plaid, cut:
2½"-wide bias strips to total 200" in length

MAKING THE HOUSE BLOCKS

Press the seam allowances as indicated by the arrows.

1 Draw a diagonal line on the wrong side of the white 4½" squares. Layer a marked square on one end of the roof 1 rectangle, right sides together. Sew on the marked line. Trim ¼" beyond the drawn line. Repeat with another marked square on the opposite end of the rectangle to make roof 1 that measures 4½" × 8½", including seam allowances. Repeat for roof 5.

Roof 1.
Make 1 unit,
4½" × 8½".

Roof 5.
Make 1 unit,
4½" × 8½".

Triangle Cutting

Using the EZ Tri-Recs rulers makes cutting the triangles and half triangles for the pennants easy. To cut the white triangles and half triangles, first align the half triangle ruler on the edge of one strip and cut one half triangle. Next cut one triangle. Rotate the ruler 180° to cut the next triangle. Continue to cut and rotate. Start the next strip with the half triangle reversed and then cut the remaining triangles, rotating the ruler as needed.

Half triangle

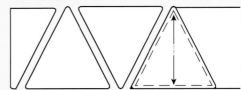

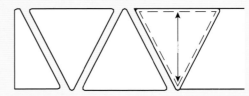

Half triangle
reversed

2 In the same manner, use the white 3½" squares and the roof 2 rectangle to make a roof that measures 3½" × 6½", including seam allowances. Repeat for roof 4.

Roof 2.
Make 1 unit,
3½" × 6½".

Roof 4.
Make 1 unit,
3½" × 6½".

3 Use the white 4" squares and the roof 3 rectangle to make a roof that measures 4" × 7½", including seam allowances. Repeat for roof 6.

Roof 3.
Make 1 unit,
4" × 7½".

Roof 6.
Make 1 unit,
4" × 7½".

4 Refer to the diagram below to join each house to a roof and, where applicable, to a white rectangle.

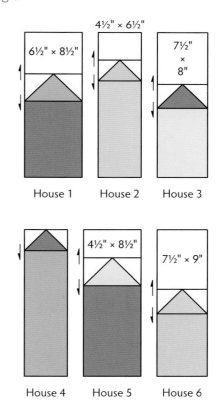

House 1   House 2   House 3

House 4   House 5   House 6

Designed and pieced by *Sandy Gervais*

TWO, FOUR, SIX, EIGHT

5 Join the houses in a row that measures 21½" × 42½", including seam allowances.

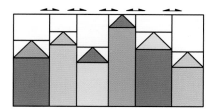

Make 1 row,
21½" × 42½".

ASSEMBLING THE QUILT

1 Sew the pennant triangles and half triangles together as shown to make the top pennant border that measures 6½" × 42½", including seam allowances.

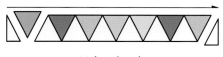

Make 1 border,
6½" × 42½".

2 Join the two white 21½" × 24½" rectangles along the long ends to make the middle section.

3 Refer to the quilt assembly diagram to join the top pennant border, middle section, and house row. The quilt top should measure 42½" × 51½".

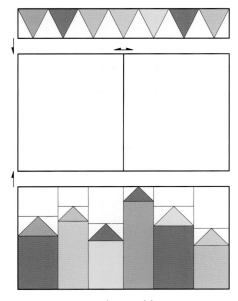

Quilt assembly

Sandy
GERVAIS

She's got spirit; can you hear it? You've got spirit; let us hear it! We love where **Sandy Gervais** went with the challenge to use FQs. We're all atwitter. We're naming Sandy captain of the Bird-Watchers Club!

If I'm perusing fat quarters in a quilt shop, I'm likely to purchase four to six, and more often than not they'll be red!

If quilting were a team sport, I'd be captain of the Cutting Team.

When it's game time in my sewing room and I have to get serious about quilting, my go-to snack is chocolate.

Share the place you were most likely to be spotted in high school: Sitting in the home-ec lounge, looking at a Vogue Pattern Book. I couldn't afford a Vogue pattern at the time, but I loved looking at them.

Two, four, six, eight, who do you appreciate when it comes time to make a quilt? My seamstresses. We often have a short schedule to make six or more quilts before Quilt Market, so we form an assembly line. Someone cuts, someone sews connector squares, someone presses, and all of a sudden a quilt comes together. I couldn't do what I do without them.

Fat quarters score a perfect 10 because they're so versatile. And what's cooler than a few fat quarters tied into a bundle, or even better, a whole fat-quarter stack?

Name two, four, six, or yes, even eight things you couldn't live without in your quilting studio: A sewing machine (I can't imagine hand piecing), a rotary cutter, a needle threader, and of course a seam ripper!

 PiecesFromMyHeart.net

4 Using your preferred appliqué method and the patterns on page 40, appliqué the bird, beak, and legs to the top of house 4. Sandy used turned-edge appliqué on her quilt. If using fusible appliqué, reverse the images before fusing.

FINISHING THE QUILT

For more details on any of the finishing steps, go to ShopMartingale.com/HowtoQuilt to download free illustrated information.

1 Layer the quilt top, batting, and backing; baste the layers together.

2 Quilt by hand or machine. The quilt shown is machine quilted with a cloud meander in the white background, Vs in the pennant border and roofs, straight vertical lines in houses 1, 3, and 5, and straight horizontal lines in houses 2, 4, and 6. Houses 1 and 3 each have two windows and a door quilted on them.

3 Trim the excess batting and backing. Use the plaid 2½"-wide bias strips to make double-fold binding, and then attach the binding to the quilt.

4 Sew the button on the bird for the eye. If the quilt will be used by a baby or small child, you can omit the button as it can be a choking hazard. You can either draw the eye on with a permanent marking pen, fuse a small circle of black fabric to the bird and stitch it in place to secure, or embroider an eye using satin stitches.

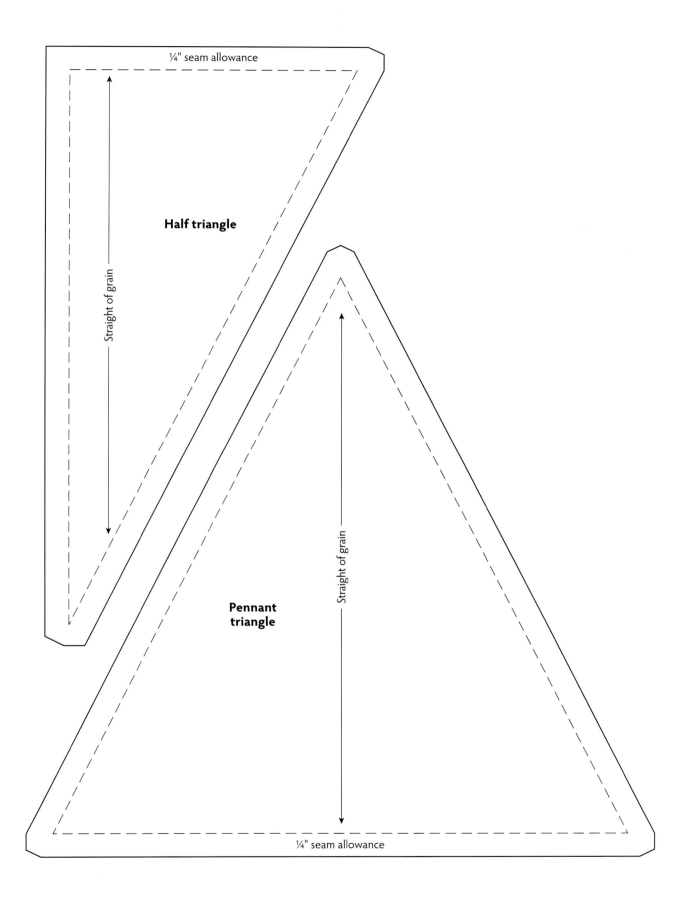

¼" seam allowance

Half triangle

Straight of grain

Pennant triangle

Straight of grain

¼" seam allowance

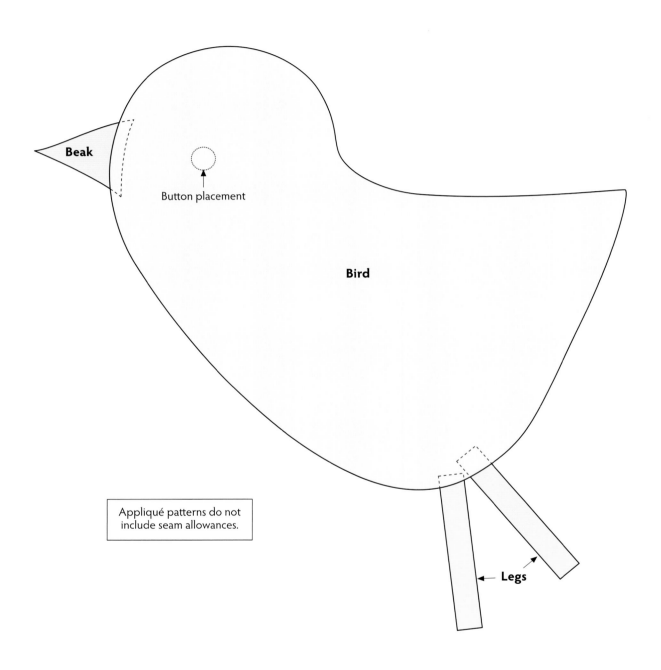

Beak

Button placement

Bird

Appliqué patterns do not
include seam allowances.

Legs

Armchair QB

BRENDA RIDDLE

3 2 FAT QUARTERS

FINISHED QUILT
74" × 74"

FINISHED BLOCK
8" × 8"

You might think QB stands for quarterback. But here's a quilterly secret—it's an armchair Quilt Beauty! Brenda calls the shots when it comes to making her quilt top sparkle. How? It's all about where she places the light, medium, and dark values. With the darker grays at the center of each quadrant and the lighter tones surrounding them, each quilt section truly radiates!

MATERIALS

Yardage is based on 42"-wide fabric. Fat quarters measure 18" × 21".

16 fat quarters of assorted prints for blocks: 2 light pink, 2 light yellow, 2 medium gray, 2 dark gray, 4 medium green, and 4 medium blue

16 fat quarters of assorted off-white tone on tones for block backgrounds

1¼ yards of off-white print for sashing and border

¾ yard of green print for binding

4⅞ yards of fabric for backing

82" × 82" piece of batting

CUTTING

All measurements include ¼" seam allowances.

From each of the fat quarters, cut:
3 strips, 3" × 21"; crosscut into 16 squares, 3" × 3" (512 total)
2 strips, 2½" × 21"; crosscut into 16 squares, 2½" × 2½" (512 total)

From the off-white print, cut:
4 strips, 2½" × 42"; crosscut 2 strips into 2 strips, 2½" × 32½"
7 strips, 4¼" × 42"

From the green print, cut:
8 strips, 2½" × 42"

TIP

Efficient Cutting

Before cutting, pair each colored fat quarter with an off-white fat quarter, right sides together. Cut both pieces at the same time—saving time and possible confusion. Each pair of fat quarters will yield four blocks, one for each quadrant of the quilt.

MAKING THE BLOCKS

Press the seam allowances as indicated by the arrows.

1 For one block, select the following: four 3" squares and four 2½" squares from one white tone on tone, and four 3" squares and four 2½" squares from one pink print.

2 Draw a diagonal line on the wrong side of the white 3" squares. Layer a marked square on a pink 3" square, right sides together. Stitch ¼" on each side of the marked line. Cut on the drawn line to yield two half-square-triangle units. Trim the units to 2½" square, including seam allowances. Make eight units.

Make 8 units.

3 Sew a white square to a half-square-triangle unit as shown. Make four units that measure 2½" × 4½", including seam allowances.

Make 4 units,
2½" × 4½".

4 Sew two units from step 3 together, rotating them as shown, to make a unit that measures 4½" square, including seam allowances. Make two units.

Make 2 units,
4½" × 4½".

5 Sew a pink 2½" square to a half-square-triangle unit as shown. Make four units that measure 2½" × 4½", including seam allowances.

Make 4 units,
2½" × 4½".

6 Join two units from step 5 to make a unit that measures 4½" square, including seam allowances. Make two units.

Make 2 units,
4½" × 4½".

7 Arrange the units from steps 4 and 6 into two rows. Sew the units into rows; join the rows to make a pink block that measures 8½" square, including seam allowances. Repeat with the remaining pink squares to make a total of eight pink blocks.

Make 8 blocks,
8½" × 8½".

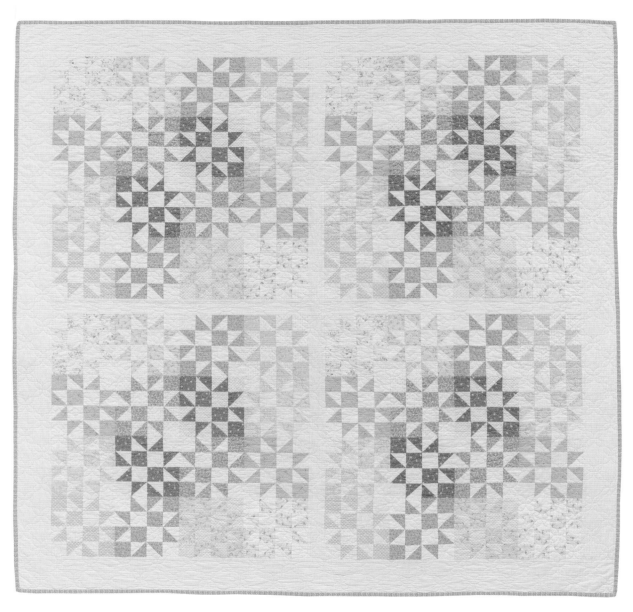

Designed by *Brenda Riddle;* quilted by *Nicole Christoffersen of Kwilt It (KwiltIt.com)*

8 Repeat steps 1–7 to make four blocks from each remaining fat-quarter color to make a total of eight yellow, eight medium gray, eight dark gray, 16 green, and 16 blue (64 blocks total).

Make 8 blocks,   Make 8 blocks,   Make 8 blocks,
8½" × 8½".   8½" × 8½".   8½" × 8½".

Make 16 blocks,   Make 16 blocks,
8½" × 8½".   8½" × 8½".

MAKING THE SECTIONS

1 Arrange a pink block, blue block, green block, and medium gray block in two rows. Sew the blocks into rows; join the rows to make section A that measures 16½" square, including seam allowances. Make eight of section A.

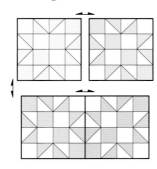

Section A.
Make 8 sections,
16½" × 16½".

We'll say it loud, because we're proud. B-E-S-T! What's it spell? BEST! Put her to the test! **Brenda Riddle** always does her best with every quilt she designs. We're naming Brenda captain of the Home Ec/Home Dec Team!

If I'm perusing fat quarters in a quilt shop, I'm likely to purchase three to six at a time.

In high school, I was voted most likely to become a dog mom (and it's true!).

If my high school had been made up entirely of quilters, they'd have voted me most likely to not follow a pattern. I make them my own.

When I have scraps left over from fat quarters, I save them in my appliqué scrap basket.

When it's game time in my sewing room and I have to get serious about quilting, my go-to snack is Ghirardelli 60% cacao baking chips.

In high school, the activity I was most involved with was the tennis team.

Now that I'm out of high school, the club I WISH quilters had today is a Binding Club! I could sit and chat and bind all day.

Two, four, six, eight, who do you appreciate when it comes time to make a quilt? My pup, who makes it his business to check out each and every step of my quiltmaking. He lounges in my studio to "keep me company," even though he's sound asleep.

Name two, four, six, or yes, even eight things you couldn't live without in your quilting studio: My studio chair, Olfa ergonomic rotary cutter (I love it!), Creative Grids rulers, a TV (usually on the Hallmark Channel), my Juki sewing machine, and beautiful Moda fabrics.

 BrendaRiddleDesigns.com

2 Arrange a green block, yellow block, dark gray block, and blue block in two rows. Sew the blocks into rows; join the rows to make section B that measures 16½" square, including seam allowances. Make eight of section B.

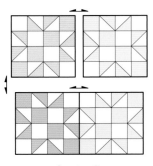

Section B.
Make 8 sections,
16½" × 16½".

ASSEMBLING THE QUILT TOP

1 Arrange two of section A and two of section B in two rows, positioning the gray blocks toward the center. Sew the sections into rows; join the rows to make a quadrant that measures 32½" square, including seam allowances. Repeat to make four quadrants.

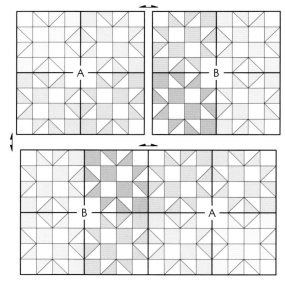

Make 4 quadrants,
32½" × 32½".

2 Sew two off-white 2½" × 42" strips together end to end. Cut this strip to 66½" long.

3 Referring to the quilt assembly diagram below, arrange the quilt quadrants, two off-white 2½" × 32½" strips, and the off-white 2½" × 66½" strip into three rows. Sew the pieces into rows; join the rows. The quilt center should measure 66½" square, including seam allowances.

4 Sew the off-white 4¼" × 42" strips together end to end. Cut two strips, 66½" long, and sew these to opposite sides of the quilt top. Press the seam allowances toward the border. Cut two strips, 74" long, and sew these to the top and bottom of the quilt. Press the seam allowances toward the border. The quilt top should measure 74" square.

FINISHING THE QUILT

For more details on any of the finishing steps, go to ShopMartingale.com/HowtoQuilt to download free illustrated information.

1 Layer the quilt top, batting, and backing; baste the layers together.

2 Quilt by hand or machine. The quilt shown is machine quilted with a pumpkin-seed pattern.

3 Trim the excess batting and backing. Use the green 2½"-wide strips to make double-fold binding, and then attach the binding to the quilt.

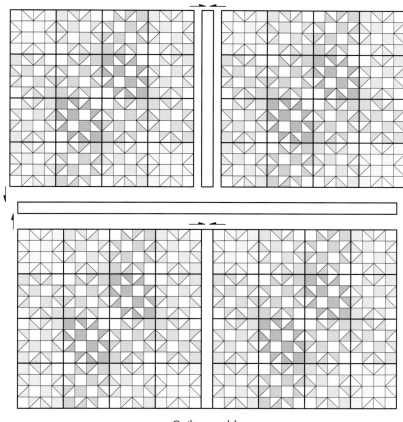

Quilt assembly

Game, Set, Match

LYNNE HAGMEIER

0 4

FAT QUARTERS

FINISHED QUILT
30½" × 30½"

We love, love the easy stitch-and-flip triangles used to make quick work of the piecing for this small wall quilt. Advantage, quilters! There's very little waste, and you'll be able to make the most of your favorite fat quarters. Partner four FQs and a background with one dominant color that forms the X, and you'll have a winner!

MATERIALS

Yardage is based on 42"-wide fabric. Fat quarters measure 18" × 21".

4 fat quarters, 1 *each* of red, orange, gold, and purple prints, for units and border
⅝ yard of tan print for units
½ yard of black print for squares and binding
1 yard of fabric for backing
35" × 35" piece of batting

CUTTING

All measurements include ¼" seam allowances.

From *each* of the fat quarters, cut:
2 strips, 2½" × 21" (8 total)
18 squares, 3" × 3" (72 total)

From the tan print, cut:
72 squares, 3" × 3"

From the black print, cut:
4 strips, 2½" × 42"
29 squares, 2½" × 2½"

MAKING THE HALF-SQUARE-TRIANGLE UNITS

Press the seam allowances as indicated by the arrows.

1 Draw a diagonal line on the wrong side of the tan squares. Layer a marked square on a red square, right sides together. Stitch ¼" on each side of the marked line. Cut on the drawn line to make two half-square-triangle units. Trim each unit to 2½" square, including seam allowances. Repeat to make 36 red/tan units.

Make 36 units.

Designed by *Lynne Hagmeier;* quilted by *Joy Johnson*

2 Repeat step 1 to make 36 orange/tan units, 36 gold/tan units, and 36 purple/tan units. Trim all units to 2½" square.

Make 36 of each unit,
2½" × 2½".

ASSEMBLING THE QUILT TOP

1 Referring to the quilt assembly diagram below, arrange the half-square-triangle units and 25 black squares in 13 rows of 13 pieces each. Pay careful attention to the unit placement and orientation. Sew the pieces into rows; join the rows. The quilt center should measure 26½" square, including seam allowances.

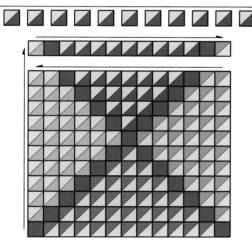

Quilt assembly

2 Sew the two gold strips together end to end. Trim to 26½" long. Repeat with the orange, purple, and red strips.

V-I-C-T-O-R-Y! That's the KTQ battle cry (if Kansas Troubles Quilters had a battle cry, that is)! **Lynne Hagmeier** is living her best life in rural Kansas. We're naming Lynne captain of the Barn Quilts Club!

In high school, I was voted most likely to move far away. (I now live five blocks from where I grew up.)

If my high school had been made up entirely of quilters, they'd have voted me most likely to break the rules.

When I have scraps left over from fat quarters, I cut them into smaller squares and strips and sort them in baskets.

If quilting were a team sport, I'd be captain of the Layered Patchwork Club.

When it's game time in my sewing room and I have to get serious about quilting, my go-to snack is cheddar crackers or popcorn.

In high school, the activities I was most involved with were drama and cheerleading.

Share the place you were most likely to be spotted in high school: On the sidelines, leading cheers.

Two, four, six, eight, who do you appreciate when it comes time to make a quilt? My machine quilter rocks!

Name two, four, six, or yes, even eight things you couldn't live without in your quilting studio: Quilters Select tools, including a rotary cutter, rulers, and mats. I also need a good light and a comfy chair.

 KTQuilts.com

3 Sew the gold border strip to the left side of the quilt center, corresponding to the gold/tan half-square-triangle units, and sew the orange border strip to the right side. Sew a remaining black square to each end of the purple and red strips, and then sew the purple border strip to the top of the quilt top and the red border strip to the bottom. The quilt top should measure 30½" square.

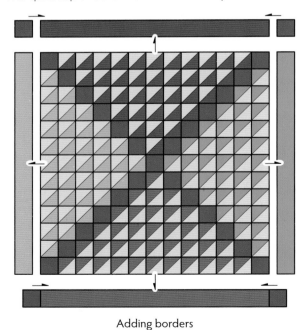

Adding borders

FINISHING THE QUILT

For more details on any of the finishing steps, go to ShopMartingale.com/HowtoQuilt to download free illustrated information.

1 Layer the quilt top, batting, and backing; baste the layers together.

2 Quilt by hand or machine. The quilt shown is machine quilted with serpentine lines in the tan triangles and swirls in the border.

3 Trim the excess batting and backing. Use the black 2½"-wide strips to make double-fold binding, and then attach the binding to the quilt.

Sweet Victory

ANNE SUTTON

04 FAT QUARTERS

FINISHED TABLE RUNNER
16½" × 51½"

Checks will definitely mark the spot where snacks are served at your next event. Whether it's a solo hopscotch session or softball season you're celebrating at your house, the tiny embroideries are the ideal finishing touch to a satisfyingly sweet table runner. Stitch 'er up!

MATERIALS

Yardage is based on 42"-wide fabric. Fat quarters measure 18" × 21".

2 fat quarters, 1 *each* of red prints A and B, for table-runner center and binding
1 fat quarter of cream print A for table-runner center
1 fat quarter of cream print B for table-runner center and inner border
⅜ yard of red print C for outer border and binding
1½ yards of white solid for embroidered blocks and backing
20" × 54" piece of batting
6-strand embroidery floss in red
Fabric pencil or water-soluble marker
Light box (optional)

CUTTING

All measurements include ¼" seam allowances.

From *each* of red prints A and B, cut:
36 squares, 2½" × 2½" (72 total)
2 strips, 2¼" × 21" (4 total)

From cream print A, cut:
30 squares, 2½" × 2½"

From cream print B, cut:
34 squares, 2½" × 2½"
2 strips, 2" × 16½"

From red print C, cut:
1 strip, 6½" × 42"; crosscut into 2 strips, 6½" × 16½"
2 strips, 2¼" × 42"

From the white solid, cut *lengthwise*:
1 piece, 20" × 54"
8 squares, 5" × 5"

ADDING THE EMBROIDERY

The embroidery patterns are on page 57.

1 Use a light box or window to trace one of each bird and two *each* of the remaining embroidery motifs onto the center of the white squares.

2 Using two strands of floss, embroider the starflowers, daisies and leaves, hearts, and birds with a backstitch or stem stitch. Stitch French knots for the eye of each bird and for the starflower centers. Use a straight stitch for the center lines of the daisies.

3 When embroidery is complete, trim the squares to 2½", centering the motifs.

ASSEMBLING THE TABLE RUNNER

Press the seam allowances as indicated by the arrows.

1 Referring to the table-runner assembly diagram below, arrange the red and cream 2½" squares in 18 rows of eight squares each. Place the embroidered white squares in place of some of the cream squares. Notice in Anne's runner that the motifs run in different directions—they do not all face the same way.

2 Sew the squares into rows; join the rows. The table-runner center should measure 16½" × 36½", including seam allowances.

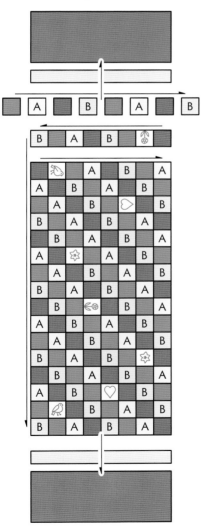

Table-runner assembly

WHAT'S THAT YOU SAY?

Anne SUTTON

Her team is red, red hot! Once she starts, she can't be stopped! And who would want to slow **Anne Sutton** down anyway? We're captivated by her style and big ideas for what's ahead. That's why we're naming Anne captain of the Dream Team!

If my high school had been made up entirely of quilters, they'd have voted me most likely to take on any craft that was out there.

When it's game time in my sewing room and I have to get serious about quilting, my go-to snack is currently Triscuits and cheese, but I go through different stages all the time.

In high school, the activity I was most involved with was Ski Club. I got to intermediate level, but my family would never believe that now.

Now that I'm out of high school, the club I WISH quilters had today is the Fabric Hoarders Club!

Share the place you were most likely to be spotted in high school: In the gym or in a classroom, working on making decorations for events. If it involved crepe paper or colored paper, I was there.

Two, four, six, eight, who do you appreciate when it comes time to make a quilt? My hubby, for cooking dinner while I work. He's a great cook.

Fat quarters score a perfect 10 because they're just the right size for so many projects, and they look so pretty in a stack. Pure inspiration!

Name two, four, six, or yes, even eight things you couldn't live without in your quilting studio: Tons of pens and pencils, my wool pincushion, pink rotary cutter, appliqué scissors, dogs, and a cup of tea.

 BunnyHillDesigns.com

Designed by *Anne Sutton;* pieced by *Nancy Ritter;*
quilted by *Rebecca Hubel*

3 Sew a cream B 2" × 16½" strip to each short end of the table-runner center, and then add a red C 6½" × 16½" rectangle to each end. The table runner should measure 16½" × 51½".

FINISHING THE TABLE RUNNER

For more details on any of the finishing steps, go to ShopMartingale.com/HowtoQuilt to download free illustrated information.

1 Layer the runner top, batting, and backing; baste the layers together.

2 Quilt by hand or machine. The table runner shown is machine quilted with diagonal lines through the cream squares and a braid with a square-in-a-square design in the red border.

3 Trim the excess batting and backing. Use the red A, B, and C 2¼"-wide strips to make double-fold binding, and then attach the binding to the table runner.

Bird 1

Bird 2

Daisy

Heart

Starflower

Embroidery Key
● French knot
— Stem stitch

Individual Medley

BRIGITTE HEITLAND

10

FAT QUARTERS

FINISHED QUILT
36½" × 36½"

FINISHED BLOCK
3" × 3"

Come on in, the water's fine! One repeat shape takes on a cool new look. It's a stroke of genius! Brigitte's careful color and value placement come together swimmingly to create an energetic off-center diamond motif. And those freestyle splashes of color keep your eye moving around this vivid wall hanging.

MATERIALS

Yardage is based on 42"-wide fabric. Fat quarters measure 18" × 21".

10 assorted fat quarters: 1 gold, 1 red, 1 light gray, 1 medium gray, 1 dark gray, 1 dark pink, 2 aqua, and 2 teal for blocks

⅜ yard of gold solid for binding

1¼ yards of fabric for backing

40" × 40" piece of batting

CUTTING

All measurements include ¼" seam allowances.

From *each* of the gold, red, and dark pink prints, cut:

14 squares, 4" × 4"; cut each square in half diagonally to yield 28 triangles (84 total)

From *each* of the light gray and medium gray prints, cut:

15 squares, 4" × 4"; cut each square in half diagonally to yield 30 triangles (60 total)

From the dark gray print, cut:

13 squares, 4" × 4"; cut each square in half diagonally to yield 26 triangles

From *each* of the aqua and teal prints, cut:

15 squares, 4" × 4"; cut each square in half diagonally to yield 30 triangles (120 total; 1 of each color will be extra)

From the gold solid, cut:

4 strips, 2½" × 42"

MAKING THE BLOCKS

1 Sew a gold triangle and a teal triangle together as shown to make a Half-Square-Triangle block. Trim the block to measure 3½" square, including seam allowances. Make 13 blocks.

3½"

3½"

Unit A.
Make 13 blocks.

Designed by *Brigitte Heitland*; pieced by *Sarah Huechteman*; quilted by Maggi Honeyman

TWO, FOUR, SIX, EIGHT

2 Repeat step 1 to make the necessary number of blocks B–O in the fabric combinations shown. Square up all blocks to measure 3½" square, including seam allowances.

Block B,
red/aqua.
Make 10.

Block C,
teal/med. gray.
Make 14.

Block D,
aqua/lt. gray.
Make 15.

Block E,
gold/aqua.
Make 12.

Block F,
teal/red.
Make 13.

Block G,
med. gray/aqua.
Make 11.

Block H,
teal/lt. gray.
Make 10.

Block I,
dk. pink/aqua.
Make 11.

Block J,
dk. pink/dk. gray.
Make 8.

Block K,
dk. gray/lt. gray.
Make 5.

Block L,
teal/dk. pink.
Make 9.

Block M,
red/dk. gray.
Make 5.

Block N,
dk. gray/med. gray.
Make 5.

Block O,
gold/dk. gray.
Make 3.

What's that you say?

Brigitte HEITLAND

First and 10! Do it again! **Brigitte Heitland** of Zen Chic went beyond 2, 4, 6, or 8 FQs—she used 10 to make her brilliant quilt. Because she's an overachiever, we're naming Brigitte captain of the Accelerated Students Squad!

If I'm perusing fat quarters in a quilt shop, I'm likely to purchase a high-quality bundle of modern-looking fabrics with a cool color scheme.

If my high school had been made up entirely of quilters, they'd have voted me most likely to create the most modern quilt layouts.

When I have scraps left over from fat quarters, I mix low-volume fabrics together and make a nice half-square-triangle pillow.

When it's game time in my sewing room and I have to get serious about quilting, my go-to snacks are apple slices.

In high school, the activity I was most involved with was orchestra. I played the flute, although I wasn't very good.

Now that I'm out of high school, the club I WISH quilters had today is a Color Play Club, with baskets of colorful scraps to put all kinds of color schemes together!

Two, four, six, eight, who do you appreciate when it comes time to make a quilt? I really rely on the helping hands of friends to assist with piecing and sewing. That way, I can spend more time designing and quilting.

Fat quarters score a perfect 10 because they let you buy a wide range of fabric prints and colors, in a size that's easy to work with, at a price that doesn't break the budget.

BrigitteHeitland.de

ASSEMBLING THE QUILT

Referring to the quilt assembly diagram below, arrange the blocks in 12 rows of 12 blocks each, noting the block letters and orientation. Sew the blocks into rows; join the rows. The quilt top should measure 36½" square.

FINISHING THE QUILT

For more details on any of the finishing steps, go to ShopMartingale.com/HowtoQuilt to download free illustrated information.

1 Layer the quilt top, batting, and backing; baste the layers together.

2 Quilt by hand or machine. The quilt shown is machine quilted with parallel lines stitched ½" from the diagonals in the blocks, which creates the effect of them radiating out from the off-center diamond.

3 Trim the excess batting and backing. Use the gold solid 2½"-wide strips to make double-fold binding, and then attach the binding to the quilt.

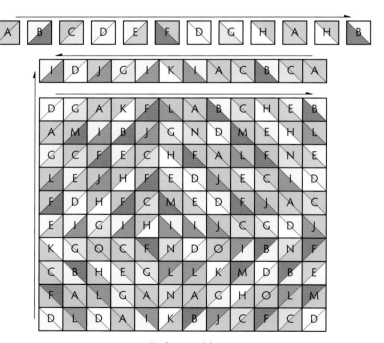

Quilt assembly

Home Run

COREY YODER

0 2
FAT QUARTERS

FINISHED PILLOW
16" × 16"

Round the bases after you stitch up a darling patchwork gingham pillow! Sweet appliquéd blossoms and big-stitch quilting finish the look, which is sure to be a winner in your home. Warning: you may have to make more than one! Otherwise, watch for a "steal" into someone's bedroom when you're not looking.

Designed and quilted
by *Corey Yoder*

MATERIALS

Yardage is based on 42"-wide fabric. Fat quarters measure 18" × 21".

2 fat quarters: 1 red print and 1 pink print for pieced squares, flower appliqués, and pillow backing
¼ yard of white solid for pieced squares and border
¼ yard of pink stripe for binding
Scrap of green print for leaf appliqués
18" × 18" square of muslin for pillow-top backing
18" × 18" piece of batting
¼ yard of paper-backed fusible web
Coordinating thread for machine appliqué
Size 8 pearl cotton in green for hand quilting
16" × 16" pillow form

CUTTING

All measurements include ¼" seam allowances.

From the red print, cut:
1 rectangle, 11½" × 16½"
36 squares, 1½" × 1½"

From the pink stripe, cut:
2 strips, 2¼" × 42"

Continued on page 65

Continued from page 63

From the white solid, cut:

2 strips, 3" × 42"; crosscut into:
  2 strips, 3" × 16½"
  2 strips, 3" × 11½"
1 strip, 1½" × 42"; crosscut into 25 squares,
  1½" × 1½"

From the pink print, cut:*

1 rectangle, 11½" × 16½"
60 squares, 1½" × 1½"

You'll need every bit of your pink fabric. See the cutting diagram below to make the best use of your fat quarter.

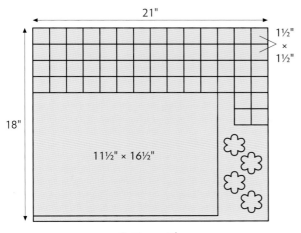

Cutting guide

MAKING THE PILLOW TOP

Press the seam allowances as indicated by the arrows.

1 Arrange the red, pink, and white squares in 11 rows of 11 squares. Odd-numbered rows alternate red and pink squares; even-numbered

rows alternate pink and white squares. Sew the squares into rows; join the rows. The pillow top should measure 11½" square, including seam allowances.

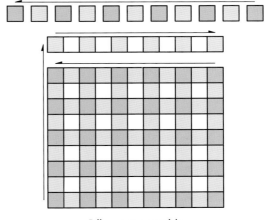

Pillow-top assembly

HOME RUN

We've got spirit, yes we do! She's got spirit, how 'bout you? **Corey Yoder** is always wearing a smile when we see her. So, we're naming Corey captain of our Good Spirits Squad!

In high school, I was voted most likely to become a lawyer.

If my high school had been made up entirely of quilters, they'd have voted me most likely to plan monthly fabric-buying and quilt-shop-visiting reunions. Forget this 5-year, 10-year reunion stuff. We'd get together monthly!

If quilting were a team sport, I'd be captain of the Easily-Distracted-by-Pretty-Fabric Team.

In high school, the activity I was most involved with was Ski Club.

Now that I'm out of high school, the club I WISH quilters had today is the Stitch & Dish Club! Isn't that a great name? Basically, stitching and chatting, two things quilters do best.

Share the place you were most likely to be spotted in high school: On the stage for band, choir, or drama.

Two, four, six, eight, who do you appreciate when it comes time to make a quilt? Everybody and everything that allows me to do what I love!

Fat quarters score a perfect 10 because I can buy a whole line of fabric without breaking the bank.

Name two, four, six, or yes, even eight things you couldn't live without in your quilting studio: Clearly Perfect Angles seam guide, my Juki sewing machine, Clover thread-cutter pendant, Olfa 60 mm rotary cutter, cutting station, ironing station, and Moda fabric.

 CorianderQuilts.com

2 Sew the white 3" × 11½" rectangles to opposite sides of the pillow top. Sew the white 3" × 16½" rectangles to the top and bottom. Press the seam allowances toward the white. The pillow top should measure 16½" square, including seam allowances.

APPLIQUÉING THE BORDER

The flower and leaf appliqué patterns are on page 67.

1 Trace 12 flowers and eight leaves onto the paper side of the fusible web. Cut the shapes apart, leaving approximately ¼" around each shape.

2 Fuse the shapes to the back of the appropriate fabrics: four pink flowers, eight red flowers, and eight green leaves. Cut out each shape and remove the paper backing.

3 Referring to the appliqué placement diagram, arrange and fuse one pink flower, two red flowers, and two green leaves to the white border on each side of the pillow. Use a machine blanket stitch or your preferred stitch to finish the edges of the appliqués.

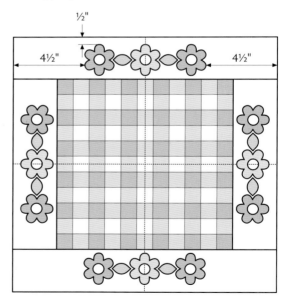

Appliqué placement

FINISHING THE PILLOW

For more details on any of the finishing steps, go to ShopMartingale.com/HowtoQuilt to download free illustrated information.

1 Layer the pillow top, batting, and muslin; baste the layers together.

2 Quilt by hand or machine. In the pillow shown, Corey used green pearl cotton to hand quilt diagonal lines through the squares and outline quilt around the pillow center. Trim the excess batting and backing so the pillow top is 16½" square.

3 Hem the red 11½" × 16½" rectangle by first folding over one long edge ¼"; press. Fold over ¼" again and sew to secure. Repeat with the pink 11½" × 16½" rectangle.

4 Lay the quilted pillow top wrong side up. Align the backing pieces from step 3, right sides up with the red rectangle on top, on the pillow top, aligning the raw edges and overlapping the hemmed edges in the center as shown. Machine baste approximately ⅛" from the edges.

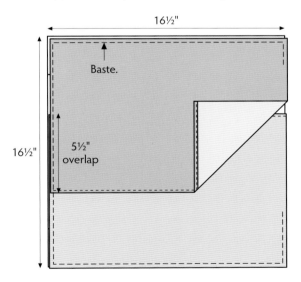

16½"

Baste.

16½"

5½" overlap

5 Use the pink 2¼"-wide strips to make double-fold binding, and then attach the binding to the pillow. Insert the pillow form.

> Appliqué patterns do not include seam allowances.

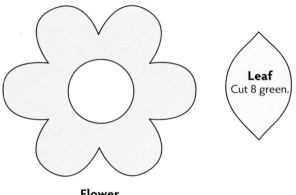

Leaf
Cut 8 green.

Flower
Cut 8 red and 4 pink.

Game Ready

JANET CLARE

04

FAT QUARTERS

FINISHED BAG
16" × 16"
(excluding handles)

FINISHED BLOCKS
4" × 4"

Designed and quilted
by *Janet Clare*

When the weather turns cool and you're off to sit in the stands, don't forget to grab your tote filled with game-ready supplies. You know the kind we're talking about—a thermos filled with your favorite warm beverage, a scarf, and maybe a little sewing project too. Practical but pretty, this is the perfect bag for the job!

MATERIALS

Yardage is based on 42"-wide fabric. Fat quarters measure 18"×21".

4 fat quarters of assorted prints for bag exterior:
    2 cream (A and B), 1 medium blue, and 1 indigo
½ yard of fabric for lining
20" × 40" piece of batting
1 pair of 21" faux leather soft bag handles

CUTTING

All measurements include ¼" seam allowances.

From cream print A, cut:
32 squares, 2⅞" × 2⅞"*

From cream print B, cut:
6 squares, 4⅞" × 4⅞"
4 squares, 2⅞" × 2⅞"
4 squares, 2½" × 2½"

From the medium blue print, cut:
2 rectangles, 6½" × 8½"
6 squares, 4⅞" × 4⅞"
4 squares, 2⅞" × 2⅞"
4 squares, 2½" × 2½"

From the indigo print, cut:
32 squares, 2⅞" × 2⅞"*

From the batting, cut:
2 squares, 20" × 20"

From the lining fabric, cut:
1 strip, 16½" × 42"; crosscut into 2 squares,
    16½" × 16½"

*Janet cut all 32 squares from one fat quarter, but to do so, you need to use either the entire width or length of the fabric. If your fabric measures slightly smaller than 18"×21", you may need two fat quarters.

MAKING THE PINWHEEL BLOCKS

Press the seam allowances as indicated by the arrows.

1 Draw a diagonal line on the wrong side of the cream A 2⅞" squares. Layer a marked square on an indigo 2⅞" square, right sides together. Stitch ¼" on each side of the marked line. Cut on the drawn line to yield two half-square-triangle units that measure 2½" square, including seam allowances. Make 64 half-square-triangle units.

Make 64 units.

2 Arrange four units into two rows. Sew the units into rows; join the rows to make a Pinwheel block that measures 4½" square, including seam allowances. Make 12 Pinwheel blocks.

Make 12 blocks,
4½" × 4½".

3 Sew two units together to make a Half Pinwheel block that measures 2½" × 4½", including seam allowances. Make eight Half Pinwheel blocks.

Make 8 blocks,
2½" × 4½".

MAKING THE HALF-SQUARE-TRIANGLE BLOCKS

1 Draw a diagonal line on the wrong side of the cream B 4⅞" squares. Layer a marked square on a blue 4⅞" square, right sides together. Stitch ¼" on each side of the marked line. Cut on the drawn line to yield two Half-Square-Triangle blocks that measure 4½" square, including seam allowances. Make 12 Half-Square-Triangle blocks.

  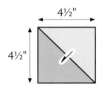

Make 12 blocks.

2 Draw a diagonal line on the wrong side of the cream B 2⅞" squares. Layer a marked square on a blue 2⅞" square, right sides together. Stitch ¼" on each side of the marked line. Cut on the drawn line to yield two half-square-triangle units that measure 2½" square, including seam allowances. Make eight half-square-triangle units.

Make 8 units.

3 Sew a unit from step 2 to a cream 2½" square as shown to make a unit that measures 2½" × 4½", including seam allowances. Make four units.

Make 4 units,
2½" × 4½".

4 Sew a unit from step 2 to a blue 2½" square as shown to make a unit that measures 2½" × 4½", including seam allowances. Make four units.

Make 4 units,
2½" × 4½".

MAKING THE BAG EXTERIOR

1 Referring to the bag assembly diagram at right, arrange the blocks and units into four rows. Sew

the pieces into rows; join the rows to make the bag front that measures 16½" square, including seam allowances. Repeat to make the bag back.

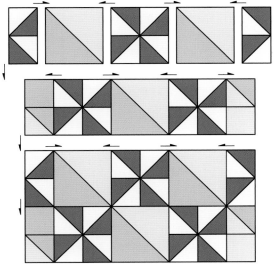

Bag assembly

Let's go, let's go, L-E-T-S . . . G-O! And let's take along **Janet Clare** and her cute-as-can-be tote bag! We're naming Janet captain of our All-England Club!

If I'm perusing fat quarters in a quilt shop, I'm likely to purchase four.

When I have scraps left over from fat quarters, I use them to make string blocks.

If quilting were a team sport, I'd be captain of the Our-Points-Don't-Always-Match-and-We-Don't-Care Club.

When it's game time in my sewing room and I have to get serious about quilting, my go-to snacks are jelly sweets and coffee.

In high school, the activities I was most involved with were orchestra and swing band. I played the clarinet.

Now that I'm out of high school, the club I WISH quilters had today is the "Anything Goes" Club!

Share the place you were most likely to be spotted in high school: In the music room.

Two, four, six, eight, who do you appreciate when it comes time to make a quilt? My elf, long-arm quilter and friend Carolyn Clark, who has helped me meet many a deadline and can always make me laugh.

Fat quarters score a perfect 10 because they're a versatile size of fabric and aren't expensive, so you can treat yourself to lots!

Name two, four, six, or yes, even eight things you couldn't live without in your quilting studio: Coffee, music, Betty (my dog), and my iron.

 *JanetClare.co.uk*

2 Layer one batting square and the bag front; baste the layers together.

3 Quilt by hand or machine. The bag shown is machine quilted with diagonal lines on both sides of the large triangle seams. Trim the excess batting from the bag front.

4 Repeat to quilt the bag back.

ASSEMBLING THE BAG

1 Stitch ⅛" from the bag edges (front and back) to secure the seams.

2 Layer the bag front and back, right sides together. Sew the side and bottom edges, leaving the top edge open. Press. Turn the bag right side out.

3 Fold under ¼" on each side of a blue 6½" × 8½" rectangle. Fold under again and stitch around all four sides. Repeat with the second blue 6½" × 8½" rectangle to make the pockets.

4 Center the pockets 3" from the top of each lining square and stitch around three sides, leaving the top of the pocket open.

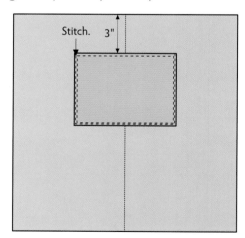

5 Layer the lining squares, right sides together. Stitch around three sides, leaving the top open and a 4" opening in the bottom.

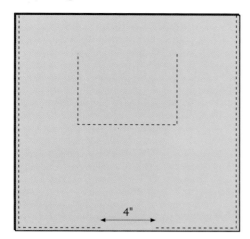

4"

6 Place the pieced bag inside the lining (right sides of the bag facing the right sides of the lining), aligning the side seams.

7 Stitch around the top of the bag. Pull the bag through the opening in the lining. Slip-stitch the opening in the lining closed and tuck the lining inside the bag.

8 Topstitch ¼" from the top of the bag to keep the lining from rolling to the outside.

9 Secure the handles in place following the manufacturer's instructions.

Swish!

SUSAN ACHE

FINISHED QUILT
58½" × 71½"

FINISHED BLOCKS
3" × 3" AND 3" × 5"

You don't have to play an up-tempo game to make a showstopping quilt. Here, the "blocks" are simple Hourglass units sewn in rows. Those rows are alternated with rows of fabric bricks, making it an easy quilt to assemble. Gather your favorite low-volume prints or mix it up and use darks. Then pump up the volume with a few brighter colors and you're on your way to a new favorite quilt. That swish sound you hear when you've finished? Nothing but net!

MATERIALS

Yardage is based on 42"-wide fabric. Fat quarters measure 18" × 21".

14 fat quarters of assorted low-volume prints (collectively referred to as "whites") for bricks and Hourglass blocks

1⅛ yards of aqua dot for Hourglass blocks, inner border, and binding

⅜ yard of green dot for Hourglass blocks

⅜ yard of gold dot for Hourglass blocks

1 yard of white print for outer border

3⅛ yards of fabric for backing

66" × 79" piece of batting

The More the Merrier!

Fourteen fat quarters of low-volume prints are sufficient for cutting all the white pieces needed for this quilt. However, if you want your quilt to be scrappier, dip into your scrap bin or stash of fat quarters and add more prints to the mix. Susan confesses to adding more to her quilt—26 prints in all.

CUTTING

All measurements include ¼" seam allowances. To cut the fat quarters, refer to the cutting guide below.

From *each* of the fat quarters, cut:

~~10~~ *8* rectangles, 3½" × 5½" (140 total; 12 will be extra) *✓Cut only 8*
4 squares, 4½" × 4½" (56 total); cut each square into quarters diagonally to yield 224 triangles *why?*

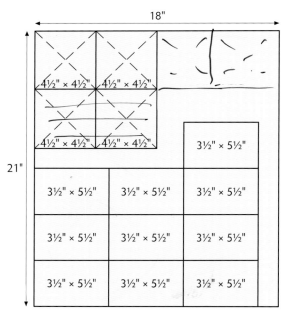

18"

21"

4½" × 4½"	4½" × 4½"	
4½" × 4½"	4½" × 4½"	3½" × 5½"
3½" × 5½"	3½" × 5½"	3½" × 5½"
3½" × 5½"	3½" × 5½"	3½" × 5½"
3½" × 5½"	3½" × 5½"	3½" × 5½"

Cutting guide

From the aqua dot, cut:

3 strips, 4½" × 42"; crosscut into 24 squares, 4½" × 4½". Cut the squares into quarters diagonally to yield 96 triangles.
7 strips, 2¼" × 42"
~~6~~ strips, 1½" × 42"

From the green dot, cut:

2 strips, 4½" × 42"; crosscut into 16 squares, 4½" × 4½". Cut the squares into quarters diagonally to yield 64 triangles.

From the gold dot, cut:

2 strips, 4½" × 42"; crosscut into 16 squares, 4½" × 4½". Cut the squares into quarters diagonally to yield 64 triangles.

From the white print, cut:

7 strips, 4½" × 42"

MAKING THE BRICK ROWS

This quilt is easy to sew, but having access to a design wall will make it easier to place the assorted white triangles in all the right places. Press the seam allowances as indicated by the arrows.

* Cut only 8 from each one. Or be sure you have 2 triangles for each 3½ × 5½ you use. You are told to cut 10 = 20 triangles. You cut only 16! What a mess this made for me.

1 Lay out the white 3½" × 5½" bricks in rows of 16 bricks each. You may find it easier to work on just two or three rows at a time, but be sure to mix up your fabrics as you go so that you aren't left with all the same prints for the last couple of rows.

2 Sew the bricks together in each row. Make eight rows that measure 5½" × 48½", including seam allowances.

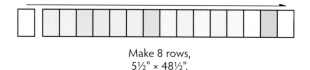

Make 8 rows,
5½" × 48½".

MAKING THE HOURGLASS ROWS

1 Using a design wall, arrange the brick rows, leaving a space for an Hourglass row between brick rows. Label the brick rows 1–8.

2 Working with brick rows 1 and 2, select two aqua triangles and one white triangle that matches the first brick in row 1. Select one white triangle that matches the first brick in row 2. Join the aqua and white triangles to make one Hourglass block. Center and trim the block to 3½" square, including seam allowances. Repeat to make a total of 16 Hourglass blocks to match the bricks in rows 1 and 2.

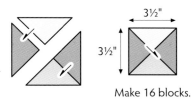

Make 16 blocks.

3 Pay careful attention and orient the white prints in each block at the top and bottom of the hourglass so they can match those in the bricks above and below it. Sew the blocks together in order to make Hourglass row A, which should measure 3½" x 48½", including seam allowances.

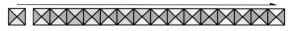

Row A.
Make 1 row, 3½" × 48½".

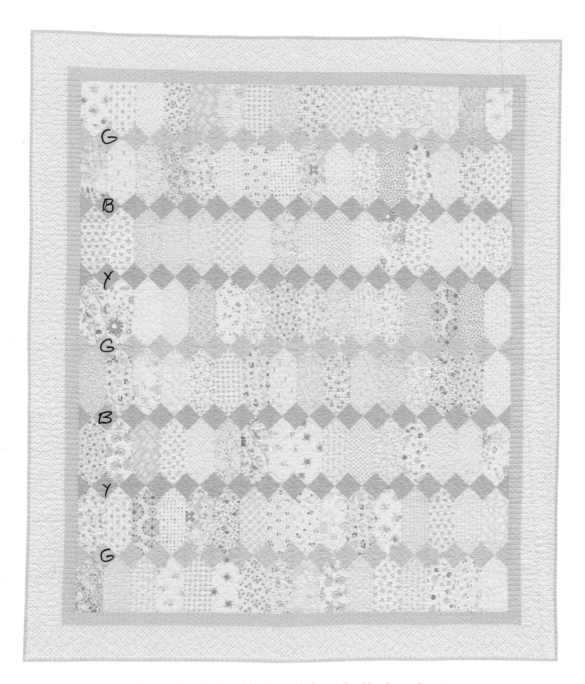

Designed and pieced by *Susan Ache;* quilted by *Susan Rogers*

4 Repeat steps 2 and 3 and refer to the quilt assembly diagram on page 80 to make six more Hourglass rows as follows:

- ❂ Row B: green triangles between brick rows 2 and 3
- ❂ Row C: gold triangles between brick rows 3 and 4
- ❂ Row D: aqua triangles between brick rows 4 and 5
- ❂ Row E: green triangles between brick rows 5 and 6
- ❂ Row F: gold triangles between brick rows 6 and 7
- ❂ Row G: aqua triangles between brick rows 7 and 8

ASSEMBLING THE QUILT TOP

1 Refer to the quilt assembly diagram. Join the rows, alternating brick and Hourglass rows to make the quilt center, which should measure 48½" x 61½", including seam allowances.

2 Sew the aqua 1½"-wide strips together end to end. Cut two strips, 61½" long, and sew them to opposite sides of the quilt top. Cut two strips, 50½" long, and sew them to the top and bottom of the quilt; press. The quilt top should measure 50½" × 63½", including seam allowances.

Scrap It Up!

If you've used extra low-volume prints for the bricks, you'll have leftover fabrics. Rather than use a single white print for the outer border, you can cut the leftover pieces into 4½"-wide strips of various lengths and piece them together to make the lengths listed on page 80 for the outer border.

3 Sew the white 4½"-wide strips together end to end. Cut two strips, 63½" long, and sew them to the opposite sides of the quilt top; press. Cut two strips, 58½" long, and sew them to the top and bottom of the quilt; press. The completed quilt top should measure 58½" × 71½".

FINISHING THE QUILT

For more details on any of the finishing steps, go to ShopMartingale.com/HowtoQuilt to download free illustrated information.

1 Layer the quilt top, batting, and backing; baste the layers together.

2 Quilt by hand or machine. The quilt shown is machine quilted with a daisy meander in the quilt center, straight lines in the aqua border, and feathers in the outer border.

3 Trim the excess batting and backing. Use the aqua 2¼"-wide strips to make double-fold binding, and then attach the binding to the quilt.

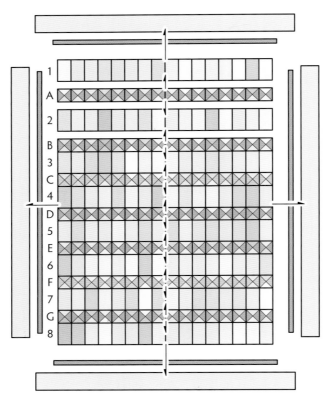

Quilt assembly